THE

PAST, PRESENT, AND FUTURE.

IN PROSE AND POETRY.

AMS PRESS
NEW YORK

THE

PAST, PRESENT, AND FUTURE.

IN PROSE AND POETRY.

By B. CLARK, Sen.,
YORK, PENNSYLVANIA.

TORONTO:
ADAM, STEVENSON, & CO., PUBLISHERS.
1867.

Library of Congress Cataloging in Publication Data

Clark, B.
   The past, present, and future in prose and poetry.

  I. Title.
PS1299.C1654P3   1974   811'.4   72-974
ISBN 0-404-00015-0

```
PS
1299           Clark, B.
.C1654
P3             The past, present,
1974            and future in prose
811 C547p       and poetry
```

Reprinted from the edition of 1867, Toronto
First AMS edition published in 1974
Manufactured in the United States of America

AMS PRESS INC.
NEW YORK, N.Y. 10003

PREFACE.

This is truly an age of progress and improvement. Without method, the following thoughts on the Past, Present, and Future, and the Poems contained in this little Work, were thrown together at such leisure moments when life's cares and duties allowed the Author to commune with himself. The only apology he has to offer for the appearance of this Work is, that it may possibly assist in swelling the tone of righteous indignation against a system of oppression, cruelty, and wrong, which has degraded a large portion of the human family, with which the writer is identified. If, by its publication, this is in any wise accomplished, the Author will patiently bear whatever criticism he may be exposed to, under the impression that the friends of humanity will not too severely deal with that which, though imperfect, is at least well intended.

B. CLARK, Sen.

CONTENTS.

	PAGE
AUTOBIOGRAPHY,	7
INTRODUCTORY,	9
PART I.—THE PAST,	11
PART II.—THE PRESENT,	17
PART III.—THE FUTURE,	21
THE FUGITIVES,	31
WEST INDIA EMANCIPATION,	35
A THOUGHT,	40

POETRY.

I.—ETHIOPIA,	41
II.—AN ACROSTIC,	43
III.—SING UNTO GOD,	44
IV.—IN MEMORIAM: ON THE LATE RIGHT REVEREND RICHARD ALLEN, FIRST BISHOP OF THE A. M. E. CHURCH,	46
V.—HYMN,	49
VI.—HAMAN,	50
VII.—LABOR,	52
VIII.—WINDS,	54
IX.—THE EMIGRANT,	55
X.—FRIENDSHIP,	57
XI.—ON SEEING A SNOW-BIRD,	59
XII.—AN ACROSTIC,	61
XIII.—TO SPRING,	62

CONTENTS.

	PAGE
XIV.—THE SLAVE-CATCHER,	64
XV.—LINES INSCRIBED TO BENJAMIN LUNDY, ESQ.,	66
XVI.—THE SLAVE-HOLDER'S APOLOGY,	69
XVII.—WHAT IS TRUTH?	72
XVIII.—PRAYER,	74
XIX.—ON THE FUGITIVE LAW,	76
XX.—ACROSTIC,	79
XXI.—THE SEMINOLE,	80
XXII.—TO MY MOTHER—LETTY WALLACE,	82
XXIII.—THE TWO FUGITIVES,	84
XXIV.—PARAPHRASE,	87
XXV.—ON JEALOUSY,	89
XXVI.—I'VE SEEN,	91
XXVII.—NO ENEMIES,	94
XXVIII.—WHAT IS A SLAVE?	97
XXIX.—ON PREJUDICE,	100
XXX.—ON BUBBLES,	101
XXXI.—BRING FLOWERS,	103
XXXII.—THE CAPTIVE,	105
XXXIII.—LINES ON HEARING OF THE BURNING OF THE STEAMER "LEXINGTON,"	107
XXXIV.—LIFE'S STRUGGLE,	108
XXXV.—THE TREE,	113
XXXVI.—ON DEATH,	114
XXXVII.—THE SLAVE'S LAMENT,	116
XXXVIII.—ACROSTIC,	117
XXXIX.—HYMN ON THE CELEBRATION OF THE FREEDOM OF THE WEST INDIES,	119
XL.—AUTUMN,	120
XLI.—ODE TO DEITY,	123
XLII.—GOD SPEED,	124
XLIII.—ODE,	126
XLIV.—THE REAPER,	127

CONTENTS.

	PAGE
XLV.—Ode,	130
XLVI.—Forget Thee,	132
XLVII.—To Write: upon being asked to Write in an Album, by Miss A. C. C.,	134
XLVIII.—Lines on the Death of a Child, J. W., aged 11 Years,	136
XLIX.—Who hath Courage?	137
L.—Years,	140
LI.—Cheer Up,	140
LII.—The Pauper's Grave,	142
LIII.—The Crisis,	144
LIV.—An Acrostic,	146
LV.—Requiescat in Pace. On the Death of Caroline Millen Clark,	147
LVI.—Pilgrim,	149
LVII.—No Energy,	151
LVIII.—Acrostic, A. C. C.,	153
LIX.—An Epitaph on my Dog Turk,	154
LX.—Do they Miss Me?—A Parody,	155
LXI.—Gossip,	157
LXII.—Love,	160
LXIII.—On the Times,	161
LXIV.—Meet in Heaven,	163
LXV.—Be Joyful: Dedicated to the First Colored Regiment of Michigan,	165

AUTOBIOGRAPHY.

THE undersigned makes no pretension to education whatever, having received but little more than one year's tuition at school in his life. Indeed, he can well remember when, in the city where he was born, an admiration would be made when one of his class would be found who could read in a newspaper. Born, therefore, in a slave State in the city of ———, of parents, on the one side, who, like many others, had the good fortune to become emancipated after more than thirty years of unrequited toil, he may well ask an apology, not only for the imperfections in this little work, but for appearing before the public in the character of an Author at all. He removed from there into the State of Pennsylvania, raised a large family of children, and during the few leisure moments that could be spared from the ordinary avocations of life, penned the Prose and Poetry comprised in this book. Not from a desire of notoriety, but having seen and felt some of the blessings of the "peculiar institution," if blessings they be; and being identified with his brethren who are suffering, in some of the States of the Union, a worse than Egyptian bondage;—an earnest desire to assist in swelling the tide of righteous indignation against a system of oppression and wrong inflicted upon a helpless and inoffensive portion of his brethren, is his only apology for appearing before the public. He is well aware that he renders himself liable to the sneers of some, and the severe criticism of others; but under an impression that what he has written may do some good, he willingly awaits the issue, and subscribes himself the public's humble servant,

B. CLARK, Sen.

THE
PAST, PRESENT, AND FUTURE.

INTRODUCTORY.

FROM time almost immemorial, the question of man's present and future existence on earth, has been, and continues to be, a matter of the deepest interest. Notwithstanding that more than eighteen hundred years have elapsed, and although we are near the terminus of the nineteenth century of the Christian era, and that more than ninety thousand millions of the human race have died, yet man's present existence and future destiny still remain shrouded in mystery. We have seen the past, we are surrounded by the present, and its indications greatly alarm us for the dark and mysterious future. It is not therefore mere idle curiosity that induces the author to publish the present work; but claiming a right to think, he claims an equal right to pen those thoughts for the consideration of his fellow-men.

In entering then upon a discussion of the past, present, and future state of the world, it is not to be expected that he would, even if he were able, give more than a mere glimpse at its history; the reader will not be surprised therefore to find many things entirely omitted, and others but partially hinted at.

PART I.

THE PAST.

IN the past history of mankind, we find what has been called the Golden Age, established by the renowned Nimrod of antiquity, whose government was styled Chaldean, and which is so graphically prefigured by the great Hebrew prophet. "God," says the prophet, "has given thee a kingdom, whose supremacy extends wherever the human race resides, so thou art that head of gold." In the land of Shinah or Chaldea stood the famous city of Babylon, founded by Nimrod about twenty-two hundred and forty-seven years before Christ. It arose to distinction under Semiramis, an African female conqueress of celebrity, and was further embellished by Nebuchadnezzar, its proud king. Its walls were three hundred feet high; it had its marble quarries, its river banks, its temple of Belus, and also its palaces and hanging gardens, constructed for the pleasure of its queen. The Chaldeans were of the African race; their shepherds acquired a knowledge of the stars while "watching their flocks by night;" and to them are we indebted for that beautiful and God-like science called astronomy. Their idolatrous lives—their licentious and voluptuous acts, will here be omitted. The length of their national existence has been variously estimated by different chronologists; let it suffice to say, that after ruling the earth, and fulfilling the great destiny of their existence,—viz., the chastisement of the chosen people of God, and their own chastisement, in their turn, for their wickedness and disobedience,—they were finally subjugated under the reign of their proud and haughty monarch, Belshazzar, by the famous Mede and Persian general, Darius, the son of Ahazuerus the Artaxerxes of the Scriptures. The Medes and Persians then became masters of the world, and governed it accordingly in their turn; but how wisely and how well, the reader may learn by referring to history, as it is not my purpose to enter into their national career from Darius down to their subjugation by the Greek general, or the "rough goat of Grecia," as stated by the same great prophet of the Scriptures. But the Greeks, under the famous Alexander, son of Philip of Macedon, then became master of the Medes and Persians. Greece soon was rendered famous for its civil polity, its learning, its military prowess, and its conquest over ancient Egypt, which thereupon became a division of its empire. Its Spartan valour is notorious; and its Olympic games were instituted fourteen hundred and fifty years before Christ. Its various kings raised Athens to an unprecedented degree of civilization. "Cadrus, the last Athenian king, abolished royalty about ten hundred and sixty-nine years before Christ." Corinth, a city of Greece, was handsomely built and beautifully adorned; and within its precincts a thousand virgins were said to be prostituted, every year, to the god Venus,—which is not incredible when we compare that city with our modern Corinths of the present day. However, it was to its inhabitants that the great Apostle of the Gentiles addressed his epistles. The destruction of Troy—the seduction of Helen— the death of Patroculus by Hector, of Hector by Achilles, and of Achilles by Paris—are important events in its history, together with many others that I cannot here mention. Until it was finally overthrown by the stern iron government, prefigured by the prophet as "a great beast arising out of the sea, having seven heads and ten horns," and having the cognomen of the Roman government, founded by Romulus about seven hundred and fifty-two years before Christ,—its history has been one of oppression, cruelty, and wrong; of conquest, rapine, war, and bloodshed. Rome proper existed as a monarchy under Tarquin and others; as a triumverate under Cæsar, Pompey, and Crassus; as a republic under the lead of Appius, Sextus, Manlius, and others; and at the time when Jesus Christ, the Saviour of mankind, made his appearance on earth, as was predicted four thousand years before, the then known world was subject to the empire, and perfectly at peace,—an unusual thing,—under Augustus Cæsar. But hail and fire, mingled with blood, was in the cup which Rome, pagan and papal, for her pride, oppression, cruelty, and wickedness, was destined to drink out of. The Barbarians under the celebrated Genseric, and the Goths and Vandals directed by the bold and daring Alaric, strewed devastation and death in their paths, until Rome, Corinth, Argus, and Sparta, yielded almost without resistance, and numbers of their inhabitants were saved by death from witnessing the slavery of their families, and the conflagration of their cities. Thus, while the State was exhausted and the Church distracted, "Mohammed, whose followers were taught to believe that every drop of blood shed in battle would secure eternal salvation," with the sword in one hand and the koran in the other, erected his throne on the ruins of Christianity. Thus fell the Roman Empire proper, whilst a branch of it was established on the British Island, for it is

"The blood of Romans, Saxons, Gauls, and Danes,
  Fills the rich tribute of the British veins;"

—which blood has spread over Europe, over America, and over the Islands of the Seas. From Alfred to Victoria, through a long line of kings, queens, despotisms, and tyrannies, we have seen convulsion after convulsion in almost rapid succession, "like the line of shadowing monarchs before the vision of Macbeth." So much for the Past.

PART II.

THE PRESENT.

WE now enter upon the Present; yet so intimately connected is the present with the past, and so dependent on the past is the future, that in recalling the history of mankind in the one, we shall necessarily be obliged to revert to the other. The present is "big," not "with the fate of Cæsar," or of Rome proper, but with the fate of untold millions of the human race. After a desperate struggle in the Italian governments between the people and their rulers, after years of almost uninterrupted supremacy, we find the Pope, although partially denounced by the people, still occupying the Papal throne, and kept there mainly by the interference of foreign arms. Those Popes who formerly had power to compel sovereigns and their subjects to tremble at a nod, and one of whom, in

1209, made the British King, John, get down from his throne and kiss his great toe, were succeeded, as we have seen, in these latter days, by one who was dragged to France, during her revolutionary government, to die in a common dungeon; and the present incumbent retained in power partly by the arms of the nephew of the very Napoleon who chained and imprisoned his predecessor in a dungeon as a common felon. Surely times have changed; and prove conclusively, even to the most superficial observer, that the world is not governed by blind chance, as some have falsely asserted. But we will pass by the days of Robespierre and the French Revolution, when men were taught by those paragons of piety, D'Alembert, Voltaire, Condorcet, and others, that there was no God; that death was an eternal sleep; modesty, refined voluptuousness; and even Christ himself an impostor. We throw a veil over the blasphemy of those days of 1790, and enter upon the present days of progress and refinement—of steamship, railroad, and telegraphic improvements. And here we find the governments of Europe, although really the most despotic, yet relaxing their hold upon their fellow-men, partially breaking the fetters from the necks of their serfs, bursting the chains of oppression, and ameliorating the condition of the children of men. The British, French, Turks, and Brazilians, are rivalling each other in abolishing the slavery of their subjects, and improving both their mental and physical condition. This is seen in the establishment of their evangelical societies, and conventions for religious purposes; in their ragged schools, their fairs, and exhibitions of mechanical ingenuity; their East India improvement societies, and their West India emancipating societies. Whilst Turkey shelters the Hungarian exile, England shelters the American fugitive. Thus we see the tri-colour of France, the crescent of Turkey, and the cross of St. George, shake hands together on the progressive improvement of man and the age, leaving the republicanism and the democracy of America bewildered in efforts to perpetuate their cherished and "peculiar institution," founded upon cruelty and injustice, and backed up by unholy compromises and fugitive slave laws. So much for the Present.

PART III.

THE FUTURE.

We will now enter upon the dark and mysterious Future, with which there is so much uncertainty connected, that none but those possessing the gift of prescience can, with any probability of approximating to the fact, predict what will really transpire, as

> "Heaven from all creatures hides the Book of Fate—
> All but the page prescribed, the present state."

Yet, in reviewing the dealings of Divine Providence with the children of men, we may form some opinion of the Future from the Past and the Present. That the present confused and turbulent condition of the world is ominous—that there is an uneasiness in the minds of men—a fearful looking for what is to take place amongst mankind—that old and long-established maxims are being exploded, and hitherto untried theories are daily developing themselves—that there is a disorganization in the Councils, Conventions, Assemblies, and Cabinets of the Nations—that they are professedly in favour of liberty, and at the same time are sustaining a system of slavery,—are facts that will scarcely be controverted. It may be said however, that this jarring of the political elements—this convulsed state of the civil and ecclesiastical world, is but the precursor of a better day,—an indication of the progressive state of the age in this, the nineteenth century, —a greater development of the march of mind, —the harbinger of the "good time coming," "when righteousness shall prevail and cover the earth," when the "leopard shall lie down with the kid," &c. But who believes that the world is any better now, or preparing to be any better, than it was a century gone by? Look at the high-handed acts of wickedness, bloodshed, and murder brought to light daily, while a paralysis so great seems to have seized both Church and State, that they may with propriety be said to be countenancing, if not, by their supineness, encouraging, almost every vice. Who then, with certainty, can predict a better state of things at any future time? No one! and "what has been is only that that will be."

But in view of the future, what will become of that large portion of the human family, comprising more than fifteen millions, partly of mixed blood, of whom we form an interesting and important part? Is there a place on this, or any other continent, spoken of in sacred or profane history, where it is recorded that they shall go, and there become a distinct and separate nation, or establish a nationality? If there be, I have yet to know it. I shall possibly be referred to Africa, and that passage of Scripture which says, "Ethiopia shall stretch forth her hands to God." I reply, that Ethiopia has done this, and will continue so to do, if, by "stretching forth her hands," in Scripture, means supplication and prayer, and not that this mixed blood of her children in America shall stand up in this, or any other locality, and there become a separate and distinct nation. After inhabiting this Continent for more than a century, both as slaves and nominal freemen, we find them here in juxtaposition with the white man—a perfect co-mixture of the Anglo-Saxon and Africo-American races—imitating all their vices, and emulating many of their virtues—embracing their habits and customs, their religion and their politics—becoming "bone of their bone, and flesh of their flesh,"—an amalgamation which has progressed until it has perfectly calicoed the country, in despite of their prejudices, (which are said to be invincible,) and their local laws, enacted expressly to prevent it. Identified as they are in practice and feeling with this nation, indeed forming part of it, will they, by any system of emigration, or colonization, voluntary or involuntary, be removed from this to any other country? We emphatically answer, No, notwithstanding the assertion of those who have injured, and therefore hate their brother, "that the two races cannot exist in the same country on terms of equality;" and colonization has become the grand panacea of the country, and prejudice its national sin. Emigration seldom, if ever, has drained a country of its inhabitants; and Ireland and Germany may be referred to as an illustration of the position advanced. *Individuals* emigrate, not *nations;* and prejudice, being but an opinion preconceived, cannot therefore be invincible. The elevation of these people is written on the page of destiny. If it were possible for them to remove from this country, it would not ultimately benefit them, nor the race among whom they might go; neither would their removal extricate this nation from the just judgments of Heaven for the great national sin of slavery. It is in this world only that nations properly are punished; and this class of persons have no right to claim exemption from punishment as the special favourites of Heaven; for they, too, are guilty concerning their brethren, either as holders, apologists, or kidnappers. But individuals of this class have gone, and others will continue to go, from this, elsewhere,—to Canada, to Africa, to the different islands of the West Indian Archipelago, and other portions of the globe. Yet this is only a proof of the migratory spirit existing within them—inherited from the race among whom they have been born, and from whom partly they have sprung— whose march has always been onward—whose desire is aggression and conquest—and whose gigantic aim is the subjugation of the earth, and control of its inhabitants. But will this class of persons remain in their present servile, degraded, and dependent condition? We think it impossible in these days of progress and improvement. They have been, and now are, receiving a practical education in the school of adversity and oppression. The time when they shall have completed that education depends upon many contingencies which may hereafter arise. There are two antagonistic principles in this country that always have been, and indeed, are now, striving for the mastery—Slavery and Liberty. One is led on by prevarication and falsehood, the other by truth—eternal truth, that divine attribute of Deity. In such a contest as this we cannot, we dare not doubt which will finally triumph,—

> "Truth, crushed to earth will rise again;
> The eternal years of God are hers."

The speedy redemption and final elevation of these people, under Divine Providence, depends mainly upon themselves. Unfortunately, our people, as a class, have not yet learnt to think that

> "Those who would be free
> Themselves must strike the blow!"

Those persons, composing a part of this great nation, will remain in these States and on this Continent, not because they are willing so to remain, but because circumstances beyond their control conspire to prevent their removal; whilst the prophet's prediction stands boldly recorded of the admixture of the "gold, silver, brass, iron, and clay" being together, constituting, as they do, a part of this great iron, or Roman government, represented as a "beast, having great iron teeth, preparing to tread down the earth;" and not content with "mere preservation, is aiming at universal mastery,"—taking possession of all parts and places of the earth, in Europe, Asia, Africa, and America, and at a thousand different points exhibiting its stern will by playing the tyrant and aggressor, tramp-

THE FUTURE. 29

ling down the earth with impunity. Agreeing with each other, yet really disagreeing—being mixed, yet separated—united, yet divided—composed of every nation, tongue, and people under heaven; thus fulfilling its great destiny, as predicted more than five thousand years gone by, until the time comes, as come it will, when the terraqueous globe that we inhabit, the solid pavement upon which we slumber, shall be burnt up; the "elastic crust, imprisoning fires that have slept undisturbed from the creation," and are now struggling to escape, daily bursting forth, exhibiting themselves in dreadful earthquakes, which scatter death and destruction in their path, shaking cities and swallowing their inhabitants, upraising islands and deluging countries, thus making preparation and gathering strength for the great and final outburst,—the last "great drama," which in the latter day will sweep the nations of every "kindred, tongue, and people" that forget God, as with a besom of destruction, and usher in the "new heavens and a new earth, wherein dwelleth righteousness."

THE FUGITIVES.

ON a bleak and somewhat dreary evening in the month of ——, near the town of ——, in the county of ——, and state of ——, about twilight were seen two weary travellers from the land of unrequited toil and oppression; one an half-blood, or familiarly termed a "mulatto," and the other of a hue somewhat more sable, sitting leisurely in a by-path by the roadside, resting their weary limbs, sorely fatigued from the effects of the previous evening's journey, and regaling themselves upon a spare and scanty meal of dry corn cake, and a drink of pure aqua that gushed from a neighbouring rivulet. Unexpectedly, like the fawn startled by the sharp crack of the hunter's rifle, or the timid hare by the sudden approach of the hounds, they were startled by the sound of footsteps, and the voice of one who, they had every reason to suppose,—from the locality, and other surrounding circumstances,—was a slave-hunter, a kidnapper; whose object was to return them back to the house of bondage from which they were endeavouring to escape, and to receive, as an equivalent for the unhallowed services rendered, the trifling reward offered by their master for their return. Their first thought was to fly as for their lives, and thus escape from one who they supposed was a betrayer; but upon discovering that the voice proceeded from one who, if not like them in situation, was at least identified in complexion with them, they concluded to stop, and listen to a proposal that he was about to make, and act as circumstances might develop themselves. The person professed unfeigned friendship and sympathy for them; and after repeated protestations, they were induced to accompany him to his domicile, and accept his proffered hospitality. They were concealed by him in a loft of the house, while the good housewife was ordered to prepare forthwith a meal of the good things of life for their accommodation and comfort. Scarcely had they been secreted in their retreat, ere they discovered the room below them filled with armed men, with ropes to pinion them, and return them back from whence they came. No time was to be lost; they soon found that they were betrayed, and determined to defend themselves to the last extremity. Snatching an old scythe from the roof, they threatened an onslaught upon the first man who should attempt to ascend the stair-way. They were summoned to surrender; and upon refusing to do so, one of the crowd ascended the ladder or stair-way, when the half-blood, with the first stroke of his weapon, nearly severed the arm from the body of the man; and with the next blow, he cut the abdomen of the second man open. The fugitives then deliberately walked down stairs, upset the supper-table that was prepared, not for them, but for their betrayers, and rushed through the panic-struck crowd undaunted and unmolested. They were pursued the next day, overtaken, confined in a stable, tied hand-and-foot, and left to ruminate over their late adventure, and unsuccessful attempt at regaining their liberty. A general jollification was carried on all night by the pursuers in the bar-room of the tavern, while the key of the stable in which the fugitives were confined was entrusted to the care of the stage driver. Sometime during the night he had occasion to visit the stable, which he did alone, when, to his astonishment, he was seized by the fugitives—who had in some way or other managed to extricate themselves,—tied hand-and-foot, and threatened with instant death if he made the least noise, or dared call for assistance. They then locked the stable door, threw the key away, and, unobserved by any one, they made a second successful and final escape.

WEST INDIA EMANCIPATION.

THE commemoration of the freedom of 800,000 human beings, who, through the providence of God, received the great blessing of immediate and unconditional emancipation on the 1st of August, 1838, should never be forgotten by us. We should perpetuate that act, as rational creatures, as lovers of freedom, and as beings connected in the great chain that binds mankind in the common bonds of brotherhood. And not particularly because coloured men were enslaved, but because they were men, and the workmanship of the great Architect of heaven and earth. Therefore, where men are oppressed, whether wrapped in the fur of the frozen Laplander, or burning under a vertical sun in the torrid zone; whether political in the battle-field, or personal in the corn-field; geographical lines, and complexional distinctions, should by no means prevent us from sympathizing with them when afflicted,—from weeping when they weep, and rejoicing when they rejoice.

To the introduction of slavery into this country, by whom, and the slave trade in general, we shall not advert. Suffice it to say, that selfishness and sordid interest, for the supposed advantage of one class of men, led to the enslavement and degradation of another class. And, for gold, they were induced to visit the coast of Africa, and there purchase, plunder, and steal the natives of that unhappy continent, and transplant them to this, to wear out a miserable existence in slavery, if happily they might escape the untold horrors of the middle passage, or survive the afflictions of acclimation in their new home of perpetual servitude. Hence we now find on the continent of North America a large class of persons of "mixed blood," descendants of Africans and Europeans, bond and free,—the sufferings of whose ancestors, in crossing the Atlantic; the slavery of themselves and their posterity in the West Indies and here; their future elevation here, as well as there, to equal civil and political privileges with their fellow-men, will, to the future historian, afford a theme thrilling and interesting. When the demon of slavery shall have been banished from society by the genial rays of Christianity and right; when the clank of the slave's chain shall no longer be heard; when the great blessing of liberty shall be alike enjoyed by all men in this otherwise free and happy country; when the oppressor and the oppressed shall become equal participants in the great blessings of civil, religious, and political privileges; then will the future historian, looking through the vista of bygone days, with a pen that glistens, and words that burn, bring to light the iniquity of the slave system, and rescue from oblivion the names of some of the noblest works of God.

Since the act of emancipation in the West Indies, the friends of the "peculiar institution" everywhere, looking through their pro-slavery spectacles at the almighty dollar alone, have denounced the act as injurious to the prosperity of the islands, as well as to the best interests of the emancipated. Overlooking or ignoring the fact, that no country ever can be so prosperous as that in which the great labouring masses become the proprietors of the soil, none will defend that soil with more avidity and zeal than its actual owners; thus rendering the country more peaceable, and more productive, in direct ratio with the increased intelligence and freedom of its population.

The day of emancipation throughout the British West Indies, was, despite the false prophets, as remarkable for quietude and solemnity, as that which marks the Sabbath in any Christian land. Disinterested travellers have declared that their behaviour, since their emancipation, has been remarkable for docility, industry, and obedience, which proves that slavery is an unnatural relation, and against the best interest of enslaver as well as enslaved. We should, then, perpetuate this great event that transpired in our midst, and return thanks to that Almighty Being, who has His "ways in the whirlwind, and whose footsteps are not seen," for this bloodless victory of liberty over oppression, of right over wrong.

> Then let us rejoice and be glad
>   When men are released from oppression;
> Let none shew a countenance sad
>   If owners give up their possession.
>
> In lasting remembrance we'll keep
>   This day, for Jehovah hath spoken,
> Although the oppressor may weep,
>   Yet fetters and chains shall be broken.

A THOUGHT.

How delightful it is to contemplate the annual return of that season of the year, ere cold and dreary winter, with hail, frost, and snow makes its appearance; when the summer has passed by, and the meridian sun hath set behind the western hills; when all nature wears a somewhat sombre aspect, and the toil of the husbandman seems about to be amply rewarded by the full harvest of mellow fruit and ripened grain; when the variegated fields, fruits, and flowers are blandly smiled upon by an Indian summer sun, and the air is perfumed with the delightful fragrance of newly-made hay, decayed fruits and flowers! How truly delightful is the contemplation of this season of the year, which gives to the eye of the beholder, the lover of nature's God, unmistakeable evidence that autumnal glory reigns alone supreme, spread by an Almighty hand!

POETRY.

I.

ETHIOPIA.

But Ethiopia hath stretch'd out
   Her hands to God on high;
And midst her many fears and doubts
   Her voice hath reach'd the sky.

And God hath heard Eth'opia's cries,
   And brought salvation near:
He promises her tears and sighs
   Shall surely disappear.

Although her sons are scatter'd wide
   O'er many distant climes,
Yet God commands that they shall bide
   His own appointed times.

If stretching forth to God her hands
    Means supplicating pray'r,
Then, from her own and distant lands,
    Her groans have filled the air.

That grace which brings salvation down
    Hath unto her appear'd;
And thousands of her sons around
    The gracious truth have heard.

And millions more in ev'ry land,
    Who've felt the heavenly love,
Join with Eth'opia's outstretch'd hands,
    To praise their Lord above.

Then stretch, Eth'opia, stretch thy hands,
    Thy God remembers thee;
And all throughout thy sunny lands,
    Declares thou *shalt* be free.

II.

AN ACROSTIC.

H ast thou, kind lady, broach'd a theme,—
A cord that's reach'd the human soul,
(R ound which there hangs a hazy dream,)
R esistlessly from pole to pole?
I ndeed, though thou art still accus'd,
E 'en when thou 'rt call'd from earth away,
T hy "Cabin" oft will be perus'd

B y thousands at some future day;
E 'en now, in almost ev'ry place,
E arnest and swift thy plea is sent,
C alling—appealing to thy race.
H ear! hear! the captive's sad lament!
E namour'd by thy sparkling wit,
R eluctant Truth has been confess'd:

S lav'ry has been pronounc'd unfit
T o be supported or caress'd!
O ur thanks we tender unto thee—
W elcome thy "Cabin" and thy "Key,"
E xposing sin and slavery!

III.

SING UNTO GOD.

Sing unto God on high,
   And to Emmanuel,
Who reigns in yonder spacious sky,
   And yet with men doth dwell.

Declare abroad His fame;
   Let ev'ry heart rejoice,
And praise the Saviour's sacred name
   With a united voice.

Dear Jesus! let Thy grace
  Be in us, and inspire
Our hearts to run the heav'nly race
  With an intense desire.

Thou art the Christians' friend
  In ev'ry trying hour;
And Thou wilt save them in the end
  From Satan's grasping power!

Then, when our work is done,
  And all our trials o'er,
Permit us to surround Thy throne,
  And praise Thee evermore.

IV.

IN MEMORIAM,

On the late Right Reverend Richard Allen, first Bishop of the A. M. E. Church.

Peace to thee, father! thou hast gone
    To that blest shore;—
Thy last great battle's fought and won;
    Thy conflict's o'er.

As dew-drops from the clouds above
    On earth distill'd,
Thy melting words, like floods of love,
    Our hearts have fill'd.

The helpless in thee found relief;
    And the distress'd
Of every kind, though torn by grief,
    Pronounce thee bless'd!

Thou lab'redst hard to teach thy race
    A Saviour's love,
And point them to that better place
    In heav'n above.

A murky light thou didst not give,
    But brilliant, clear!
Thy deeds of piety shall live
    Full many a year.

Not like a transient meteor, thou,
    But a bright star,
Whose glorious light is seen e'en now,
    Both near and far.

Loud sang the angels to God's praise
    In chorus high,   [day's
When thou hadst crowned thy lengthen'd
    In victory!

Waiting around thy couch they stood
    To guide thee o'er
The surging waves of death's cold flood,
    To Canaan's shore.

Then rest thee, father, till that day
    When saints shall rise,
And burst the bands of mortal clay,
    To mount the skies.

Thou shalt then rewarded be, and
    Thy robe so bright,
Outshine the sun throughout that land
    Of love and light.

Then in thy crown shall many stars
    To thee be given;
And all thy tears, and wounds, and scars,
    Be heal'd in heaven.

V.

HYMN.

Lord, condescend to bless us now,
Whilst at Thy feet we humbly bow;
And let Thy Spirit from above
Descend and fill our hearts with love.

Make us to feel Thy presence near,
And fill this place with holy fear.
Oh! let Thy pard'ning love be found,
And grace, and faith, and hope abound.

May sinners wonder, feel, and fear,
And tremble with a penitent tear.
May mourners now embrace Thy love,
And Christians praise Thee, Lord, above.

Thus shall we serve Thee, gracious Lord!
And walk obedient to Thy Word;
And live, and love, and hope, and sing,
Redemption to our God and King!

VI.

HAMAN.

A MONARCH sat on Persia's throne—
Whose sceptre sway'd the world alone—
  In royal state;
None dar'd his sovereign will dispute;
Around him stood his vassals mute,—
  For he was great.

Throughout the whole of Persia's land
One only dar'd approach the hand
  Of royalty.
Haman! the chieftain of that king—
Whose heart conceiv'd a wicked thing
  'Gainst Mordecai.

He issued, first, a firm decree,
That all should worship when they'd see
  His image rise.

But Mordecai, the righteous Jew,
Refus'd, as ev'ry one should do,
    To his surprise!

At length a gallows high he swung,
Upon which all were to be hung,
    As he did vow.
But as he rode, in royal state,
Sat Mordecai at the gate,
    And would not bow.

For this his wrath was kindled sore,
And at the banquet loud he swore
    He'd hang the Jews.
But Esther said,—"Before the king
I'll go, and stop this wicked thing,
    If he refuse."

The king receiv'd Queen Esther's plea,
Releas'd the Jews immediately,
    And Haman hung!

Thus on the gallows, high and new,
He'd built for Mordecai, the Jew,
    Himself was swung.

How many thousands, since that day,
Have built a gallows, so that they
    Some one could hang!
But, to their horror and surprise,
They've found, with all their deep disguise,
    Themselves have swang.

VII.

LABOR.

Occupy some worthy place,
    Care not if it soil;
Honest labor's no disgrace;
    Man was made to toil.

LABOR.

Therefore, labor ever on—
  Have an end in view,
Though you may be look'd upon
  By an idle crew.

Labor with the head or hand,
  With the heart or pen;
Labor, and you'll understand
  How to do, *and when!*

Labor, and make no complaint
  That the time is long;
Work in earnest,—never faint
  Till the weak be strong.

Labor! zealous, calm, secure!
  Aim at something high.
Hope and labor till you're sure
  Your reward is nigh.

Labor while the day is long,
  Lest the night be near.
Battle manfully with wrong,
  Till the right appear.

VIII.

WINDS.

Winds echo through the trees,
  And are unseen,
Though we may feel the breeze
  Ever so keen.

So deeds, however kind,
  When they are past,
Are driven from the mind,
  Like the rude blast.

IX.

THE EMIGRANT.

Adieu to the land of my birth—
   Proud land of the slave and the free!
What charms have thy bosom on earth
   For men of complexion like me?

In this boasted land of the free
   I've suffered contumely and scorn;
And cannot relate what I see
   Is reserved for millions unborn.

If places on earth can be found
   Untainted by slavery's breath,
I'll find them, or search the world round
   Till my sorrows are ended in death.

Thy liberty is but a name—
    A byword—a jargon, in fine!
Thy freemen of colour—oh shame!—
    Are glad to escape from thy clime!

Adieu to thy stripes and thy stars,
    That vauntingly float o'er the main!
Adieu to thy Lynch-laws and jars,
    Thy fetters, thy charter, and chain!

I go to the Isles of the Sea,
    Where men are not judged by their hue!
Where all are protected and free—
    My native land, therefore, adieu!

X.

FRIENDSHIP.

Friendship is seldom found on earth—
   At least we've heard it said—
For, when enjoying pleasant mirth,
   We seldom need its aid.

Is Friendship, then, an empty dream—
   A phantom in disguise—
A vision only to be seen
   By those of double eyes?

Or is it really felt or found
   By those in deep distress—
Like rain upon the parched ground,
   Or barren wilderness?

FRIENDSHIP.

Ye who have felt the bitter pang
    Of unrelenting grief,
Tell me, when Friendship never sprang
    To offer you relief?

When, like the solitary dove
    In woodbine, all alone,
Your pensive notes of absent love
    Have caus'd your heart to moan,—

Has not the hand of some kind friend
    Assuaged your troubl'd breast?
Has no one offered to defend,
    Or aid you when distress'd?

Is Friendship only felt at best
    Where plenty reigns supreme;
And seldom to be found the guest
    Of poverty unseen?

Oh, no! disint'rested friendship can,
   And has been found, we know—
A purer, sweeter friendship than
   This earth can e'er bestow.

A friendship that is undefiled
   Flows down from heaven above;—
Then seek it, as a little child
   First seeks its parents' love.

XI.

ON SEEING A SNOW-BIRD.

The woodman sits snug at his hearth,
   The ground is all cover'd with snow,
The foliage has gone from the earth,
   Then go, little snow-bird, now go!

The woodpecker, raven, and all,
    Have hid them secure in their hold;
And the snow yet continues to fall,—
    The weather is chilly and cold.

Thou art a precursor of ill
    To the sad, unfortunate poor;
For the snowflakes follow thee still,
    And lie cold at the poor man's door.

The swallow hath gone to the barn,
    And the cuckoo, the robin, and wren;—
Then go, little bird, when 'tis warm,
    Nor pay us a visit again.

XII.

AN ACROSTIC.

C onsistent friend of right,
H ast thou been called hence?
A rmed with power and might,
R eceive thy recompense!
L iberty's advocate,
E ver noble and great!
S oon found a wat'ry grave

F ar from thy native land.
O h! was there none to save?
L ove for the human kind
L ed thee to seek no rest!
E ngrav'd within the mind,
N ations will call thee blest!

XIII.

TO SPRING.

OLD Winter's past,
    With storm and blast,
Let's be no longer sad!
    For Spring has come,
    With all its bloom,
And earth again is glad!

The smiling field
    Its harvests yield,
The brooks with waters flow;
    Then let's rejoice
    With cheerful voice,
And on to duty go!

TO SPRING.

The joyful bird
Can now be heard
With melody to sing!
All nature, too,
Unites to view
The pleasant days of Spring.

Industriously
The stirring bee
Prepares to take his round
Among the bow'rs
And smiling flow'rs,
Where'er they may be found.

The sweetest green
Can now be seen,—
The worm begins to creep;
Then why should we
Act sluggishly,
Or waste our time in sleep?

No time to rest—
Life's short at best—
Let's work while yet we may;
With cheerful heart
We'll do our part,
Ere we be called away.

XIV.

THE SLAVE-CATCHER.

Hark! the cry,
"A slave ran by!"
Quick, pursue the track;
Don't delay—
He'll get away
Ere we get him back.

THE SLAVE-CATCHER.

I regard
The large reward
By the master giv'n;
And I go
Through rain and snow,
As by it I'm driv'n.

I am, sir,
The master's cur,
As I'm known to scout
Through the fen,
The bog, and glen,
When a slave is out.

Hark! the cry,
"A slave's gone by!"
Quick, pursue the track;
Don't delay—
He'll get away
Ere we get him back!

XV.

LINES

Inscribed to Benjamin Lundy, Esq.

Lundy! thy mighty zeal—
   Persecution!—strife!—
Call'd forth a host of friends
   Into active life.

If noble deeds could speak,
   They would tell of thee,
Who to the world proclaim'd
   Man was created free.

Thou labour'dst to secure
   Freedom in this great land,
Not only to the white,
   But to the colour'd band.

LINES. 67

But thou art called hence
    Before the battle's won;
Still with thine armour on,
    All blazing in the sun.

Although of stature small,
    Thou wert large in heart,
And for thy fellow-men
    Didst act a brother's part.

Thou didst not cease to call
    On all men to repent,
And to their brother give
    Liberty and content.

Onward! thy watchword was,
    To set the captive free,
Until, throughout the earth,
    All men shall brothers be.

See! what a host has now
    Quick rallied to the call;
And who, like thee, demands
    Full liberty for all!

Fearlessly they defend
    All those that are oppress'd,
And nobly condescend
    To succour the distress'd.

Onward! their motto is;
    Agitate! their plan;
Emancipate! their cry;
    Make the slave a man.

XVI.

THE SLAVE-HOLDER'S APOLOGY.

These slaves I now possess are mine,
    Sanction'd by laws of earth and Heaven.
We thank Thee, gracious power divine,
    That unto us this boon is given.

In Scripture thou hast bidden us make
    Slaves of the heathen and the stranger;
And if we heathen people take,
    There is no harm, and much less danger.

Slav'ry 's a system that 's ordain'd
    On earth to be, and to us given;
This can be read in language plain,
    And thus we thank Thee, Lord in heaven,

That, in Thy wisdom, Thou mad'st us
    The instruments to show Thy power,
And thus fulfil on them the curse
    Of "Cain," nay "Ham," until this hour!

What care we for the Northern fool,
    Who talks about the rights of niggers?
We know that we were made to rule,
    And they ordain'd to be the diggers.

Besides, it can be seen at sight,
    Our slaves, if freed, would turn out lazy;
And if the "fanatics" are right,
    The Scriptures' wrong, or we are crazy.

It says, old Abraham held slaves,
    And Paul sent back Onesimus:
Those patr'archs would spring from their graves
    To hear the prate of Abolition'sts!

THE SLAVE-HOLDER'S APOLOGY.

They say, "Great Britain has set free
    Some few of her poor, lazy creatures!"
But if they'd just reflect, they'd see
    They've missed the mark by many figures.

For who will cultivate the soil,
    Or plant their sugar-cane and cotton?
Their niggers now are freed from toil,
    And soon their ills will be forgotten.

Then hold on, brethren of the South—
    They tell me Abolition's dying:
This cry's in almost ev'ry mouth,
    Unless you think the rascal's lying.

Whether or not, this corner-stone
    Of our Republic shall not crumble;
Our laws and "niggers" are our own,
    So let the poor "fanatics" grumble!

XVII.

WHAT IS TRUTH?

What is Truth? said those of old,
   Who, oft warned by Israel's God,
Whose daring deeds, then all untold,
   Brought down on them the Avenger's rod.

What is Truth? was asked by one
   Whom Israel had been taught to fear,
Whilst, with scorn, he looked upon
   The very truth that was so near.

What is Truth? said Pilate, when
   The truth had reached his inmost heart
Washing clean his hands again,
   In murder, said he'd have no part.

WHAT IS TRUTH?

What is Truth? the sland'rer says—
　Is it to blast my neighbours' name;
Them defaming all my days—
　Acting as though I had no shame?

What is Truth? the tyrant said,
　Whilst he enslav'd his fellow-man:
Now my will shall be obey'd,
　For who my right will dare to scan?

What is Truth? the miser says,
　While counting o'er his ill-got gain:
What care I for her good ways,
　So I the "yellow dross" obtain.

What is Truth? the sceptic says,
　While doubt and fears annoy his path:
Shall I heed her peaceful ways,
　Or meet at last indignant wrath?

What is Truth? the Christian cries,
   Publishing a Saviour's love,
While from earth to heaven he hies—
   To the starry realms above.

What is Truth? I may not tell—
   What is "the Truth" shall be made known;
What is Truth, remember well,
   Is firm as God's eternal throne!

XVIII.

PRAYER.

Grant us, O Lord, a heart to pray,
A heart to walk in wisdom's way,
   A heart resign'd to Thee;
And while we journey here below,
May streams of peace and comfort flow
   As rivers—bold and free.

PRAYER.

Grant us a heart—true and sincere,
Endued with grace and holy fear,
    Resolv'd to love Thee still;—
To follow Thee in all thy ways,
And spend the remnant of our days
    Obedient to Thy will.

Grant, gracious Lord, whene'er we stray
From Thee, thy Holy Spirit may
    Incline us to repent.
Oh! keep us from presumptuous sin,
Let thy good Spirit dwell within,
    And give us peace—content.

Oh! grant, that we may always act
To others just and right, in fact
    As they to us should do;
That, when our time on earth shall end,
With all the good we may ascend
    The heavenly land to view.

Grant that our parents, children, wife,
May also lead a spotless life,
    While here on earth we stay;
And, oh! where'er our lot be cast,
May we remember that, at last
    We shall be call'd away.

XIX.

ON THE FUGITIVE LAW.

AND so you will not hear the prayer
Of thousands who, in common, share
Rights that are equal, just, and fair,—
    Ye've not discuss'd!
    Beware!—we warn you well!—
    For soon ye must!

ON THE FUGITIVE LAW.

None dare, ye say, dispute our claim;
Nay, more!—none shall discuss or blame
"Our sacred institution!"—Shame!
    This warning take:
      Beware!—we warn you well!—
    The laws ye make!

Your cry, so much like those of old,—
"Our time's not come!" Then cease to scold,
For, when it does, we still will hold
    This system given,—
      Beware!—we warn you well!—
    The frowns of Heaven!

Think ye can stop the march of mind?
Go,—think of chaining fast the wind!
Your "fugitive laws," all combined,
    Must cease to be—
      Beware!—we warn you well!—
    Man will be free!

ON THE FUGITIVE LAW.

The world is rack'd with many plans
T' ameliorate this state of man's,
While every nation closely scans
  Each other's ways:
  Beware!—we warn you well!—
  Your number'd days!

As certain birds prefer the night,
So tyrants always dread the light
Of Freedom! and the laws of right,—
  As well they may:
  Beware!—we warn you well!—
  The people pray!

Men, for a time, may bear the ill,
To be enslav'd at human will;
Yet, in despite of tyrants' skill,
  Will burst their chains:
  Beware!—we warn you well!—
  This truth remains!

XX.

ACROSTIC.

B old in the cause of truth;—
E ver maintained the right;—
N ot in the strength of man!—
I n God!—the infinite!
A lways consistent,—true
'M idst difficulties, strife;—
I nto the battle call'd;—
N ever despair'd through life!

L et tyrants rage the more,
U ntil their anger's o'er,—
N or let them us allure;
D ear friend! we rest secure
Y our trust in God is sure.

XXI.

THE SEMINOLE.

Bold champion of a noble race,
Who never fear'd the pale man's face,
Or nation tried'st thou to disgrace,
        Or name of Seminolé;

Who, for the rescue of thy wife,
Upraised the tomahawk and knife,
And led thy brethren to the strife,—
        'Twas the brave Oceola!

Roused by the war-whoop's distant sound,
Scatter'd thou death and carnage round
Thine everglade, or sacred mound,
        And lands of Seminolé.

THE SEMINOLE.

But, ah! the fatal moment, when
Thou placed reliance on the men,
Who, under flag of truce, did then
    Deceive thee, Oceola!

Fame will record it to the shame
Of those who plann'd, and those who came
To desecrate fair Freedom's name
    By robbing Seminolé.

But thou, Floridan, art the boast
Through thy wild romantic coast,
While all thy brave unconquered host
    Remember Oceola!

XXII.

TO MY MOTHER—LETTY WALLACE.

Mother!—we have seen thee wasting,
  Hour by hour, as time has fled,
And we sometimes fear thee hast'ning
  To be number'd with the dead.

Yet, the thought of separation
  From thee, oft disturbs our sleep,
And, with ceaseless observation,
  We, the watchful vigils keep.

Mother!—we have known thy kindness
  In our early childhood days,
When in unknown infant blindness
  We have stray'd from wisdom's ways.

TO MY MOTHER.

Mother!—we have seen thee languish,
    And have wept to hear thee sigh;
While, with pain and bitter anguish
    We could do no more than cry.

Mother!—we will smooth thy pillow
    Whilst the spark of life shall last;
"Hang our harps upon the willow,"
    Till the fun'ral train has pass'd.

We will think of thee, dear mother!
    When thou 'rt in the silent grave;
And we 'll comfort one another
    With the dying words thou gave.

Should the Lord be pleased to take thee
    From thy children, to thee given;
Oh! we pray that He may make thee
    Pure and spotless—fit for heav'n.

XXIII.

THE TWO FUGITIVES.

Hard by, within a southern clime,
There liv'd a patriarch sublime,
With slaves to tremble at his nod,
As heathens to a wooden god.

Two fav'rite slaves this lord possess'd,
(Perhaps more knowing than the rest,)
Who long desir'd to seek a place
Where slav'ry dar'd not show its face.

At length they heard that liberty
Was found beyond the States called free,
So they determined, come what may,
To leave their lord without delay.

Accordingly, as night approach'd,
Snugly ensconc'd within a coach,
They quickly left their lord's domain,
Through storm, and snow, and hail, and rain.

An hour or so had scarce gone by,
Ere there was raised a great outcry:—
"Pursue! pursue! you'll find their track—
Fly quick! and overtake the hack!"

The nags were faint—the snow was deep—
And up the hills they scarce could creep—
When, suddenly, three men cried out,
"Stop! stop that hack; turn quick about!

"We wish to know if you've white men,
Or 'niggers,' for we've come for them!
We're authorized to take them now—
Two thousand doll's are ours, we vow."

The driver, tremb'ling, soon obey'd,—
Their orders to fulfil essayed;—
The men within said, "'Tis but death—
We'll fight them while we've life and breath!"

A scuffle quickly now ensued;
With moral power they were endued.
They fired,—they missed,—they fired again,—
"Two thousand dollars" lost—and men!

The "slaves" at length a refuge found,
Until the snow had left the ground—
When off they marched for Canada,
Protected by Victoria!

XXIV.

PARAPHRASE,
Luke xxiv.

It happen'd on a summer even-tide,
Soon after Christ had freely bled and died,
Two travellers, upon the dusty road,
Each going to his own belov'd abode.

And, walking on, their conversation turn'd,
From many things, to that they just discern'd.
"Sure there are things," said one, "beyond our
    thought;
Wonders have been, this day, in Israel wrought."

They both conversed about things they had seen,
Until a stranger joined them, but unseen:
"Say, what communion is it, sirs, I pray,
Ye seem to have along this lonely way?"

"Art thou, indeed, a stranger, sir, who says,
Thou know'st not what has happen'd in these days?
How that our people did one Jesus bleed.
We thought 'twas He that would have Isr'el freed!"

"Oh fools!" said He, "ought Christ not to have died?
Foretold of yore, and by Him prophesied."
Then Moses and the Prophets He reveal'd,
Which to their eyelids heretofore were seal'd.

Then to the village, as they all drew near,
He fain would go; but, said they, "Tarry here;
The day is spent, we cannot let thee go;
More of thy name and nature we would know."

The three together straightway sat at meat:
He took, He bless'd, He broke the bread, they eat.
They saw Him ere He vanish'd from their sight:
"How burn'd our hearts within us here this night!"

XXV.

ON JEALOUSY.

What wretched thoughts disturb my breast;
Deprive me of my daily rest;
Destroy my equanimity!
"Tell me, can this be jealousy?"

Why is it that I hate to see
My neighbours in prosperity?
Why am I fill'd with misery?
"Tell me, can this be jealousy?"

Does this incline me to traduce,
To envy, slander, and abuse?
Make mountains, when they mole-hills be?
"Tell me, is not this jealousy?"

To e'en suspect, to e'en believe,
That ev'ry person will deceive,
And do some secret injury—
"Tell me, is this not jealousy?"

By inuendoes stab, beguile
A friend, yet meet him with a smile,
And make him think I'm open, free—
"Tell me, is this not jealousy?"

Oh! cruel monster, I'm thy slave—
The more I have, the more I crave;
I envy ev'ry one I see—
This—this is surely "jealousy."

XXVI.

I'VE SEEN.

I've seen, in Democratic States,
 Within the Nation's Hall,
Where Congress meets, and legislates
 About the rights of all;

A legal trade in human flesh,
 That most of men despise;
And men bought for the market—fresh!—
 Before the members' eyes.

I've seen the Southern members rave,
 And in their places swear,
Because some poor, degraded slave
 Had offer'd them a prayer!

I've seen the trafficker in blood,
  With coppels on before,
Drive by, while legislators stood
  Discussing on the floor—

Declaiming, loudly, to the world
  That all this land is free,
And, with their stripes and stars unfurl'd,
  They shouted "Liberty!"

I've seen excitement raging high
  Throughout this wide domain,
Because some slaves had dared to fly
  From slav'ry's galling chain.

I've seen in these United States—
  This consecrated soil—
Men bought and sold by pounds and weights,
  In Southern fields to toil.

I'VE SEEN.

I've seen a slave, though not by day,
    Whose back was mark'd with scars,
Unable to discern his way,
    Stand gazing at the stars.

I've seen the hunter on his track,
    And men and dogs at bay,
Determined to regain him back
    This side of Canada.

I've seen—the half I ne'er can tell,
    Of chains, and slaves, and strife;
I've seen the priest and man-thief sell
    His brother man for life.

XXVII.

NO ENEMIES.

" He has no enemies!" you say.
　　I pity his condition;
His manhood he has thrown away,
　　His candour and position.

"He has no enemies!"　Well, then,
　　The reason is,—he never
Has heart enough to act but when
　　He sees "which way's the weather."

His principles are very light,
　　If he is not contented
To be traduced for doing right,
　　When once he has assented.

NO ENEMIES.

"He has no enemies!" Indeed!
    Then what has he been doing?
Or, what on earth can be his creed?
    What has he been pursuing?

A truckling—vacillating course,—
    Unmanly, undecided;—
His little puny soul is worse
    Than sixpence twice divided!

Then give me one of upright heart,
    Who dares the truth to utter,
And act a nobler, manlier part,
    Though enemies do mutter.

A man of earnest, iron will,
    Whose enemies are many;
And yet, whose virtue, strength, and skill,
    Are undeterred by any:

Whose fearless love for truth and right
    Keeps falsehood ever distant;
And though he may be crushed by might,
    Yet always acts consistent.

Aye! like the sturdy forest oak,
    Through which the winds do rattle,
Stands firmer from the heavy stroke,
    Prepared for Truth to battle.

Such is the man, whose noble soul,
    When roused to proper action,
Disdains a sordid, base control,
    Or enemies' detraction.

Who knows, when virtue's lost or fled,
    That time is really trying;
For if the man is not then dead,
    He truly must be dying.

XXVIII.

WHAT IS A SLAVE?

A slave is—what?
A thing that's got
Nothing, and that alone!
His time—his wife—
And e'en his life,
He dare not call his own.

A slave is—what?
Ah! dreadful lot
Is his that's doomed to toil,
Without regard,
Or just reward,
Upon another's soil.

A slave is—what?
Ah! cruel thought,
That I should have to be,
In constant strife,
Throughout my life,
Deprived of liberty.

A slave is—what?
A perfect naught,
Shorn of his legal right;
And then compelled
To work, he's held,
The remnant of his life.

A slave is—what?
A being bought,
Or stolen from himself,
By Christians, who
This trade pursue,
For sordid, paltry pelf.

WHAT IS A SLAVE?

A slave is—what?
A being sought
Throughout this wide domain;
Through bog and glen,
By dogs and men,
For lucre—cursed gain!

A slave is—what?
I pray do not
Insist; I cannot know,
Nor words impart,
Or, painter's art,
Describe a slave—ah, no!

A slave is—what?
Tell I can not,—
The task I would not crave:
If you would know,
Then straightway go,
And be yourself a slave!

XXIX.

ON PREJUDICE.

WHAT green-ey'd monster now is this,
Strolling our land o'er in triumph—
With great boldness? Whence his country,
Or his home? Stranger is he, or,
Native of our land, peculiar?
Indigenous, or by whatever
Name is he known? If he be friend,
He comes in shapes most comely,
Yet most questionable; indeed,
The mark of falsehood is upon
His brow. He has and wears a face
Double—nay more, e'en his very
Judgments warped are—his eye not
Single. Reason! he hath it not!
Nor will he be reasoned with.
Yet most wilily hath he entwined

Himself among, around statesmen,
Politicians.   In sanctuaries
Hath he gone, throwing his influence
There among—corrupting, and, yea
Poisoning all the clear, pure streams
Of piety and peace.   The name
He bears is, PREJUDICE!—his home
America!—birthplace, the PIT!

XXX.

ON BUBBLES.

OFTEN, in our waking dreams,
We invent a thousand schemes,
    That bring with them troubles;
But, too late! we find, indeed,
That, alas! they can't succeed,
    And are empty bubbles.

Men are seen, with anxious care,
"Building castles in the air,"
    With an interest double;
But their fancied visions bright,
By experience brought to light,
    Are but one great bubble.

Some are preaching to their shame;
And, to get a godly name,
    Preach a language double;—
Drag the Holy Scriptures in,—
Justify the Man of Sin,
    And secure a bubble.

Men of genius, skill, and art,
Statesmen, lawyers, and, in short,
    All experience trouble,
After wasting years and health,
To procure a name, or wealth,
    Find they've but a bubble.

Then, if peace we wish below,
Our joys from Heaven must flow—
    Our exertions double;
So, when death appears in view,
We may bid the world adieu,
    With its mighty bubble.

XXXI.

BRING FLOWERS.

Bring flowers—gay flowers, to garnish the tomb,
    Where, enshrined, the poor feeble body shall rest;
Let violets and dahlias continue to bloom,—
    Be careful to keep them well dress'd.

How very desirous to select a place where,
    With fine gravelled walks, and high iron rail,
Where gay roses grow with profusion and care,
    To inter the body so frail!

'Tis well! but how many forget the poor soul
　Is vastly more lasting than poor feeble dust;
Neglect to preserve it a mansion or goal,
　With God and the holy and just.

Let flattering tombstones of marble denote
　The places where wealth is decaying to dust;
And epitaphs tell of their virtues in rote,—
　How wise they have lived, and how just.

Bring flowers—sweet flowers, to strew on the grave
　Where virtue neglected lies hid from the eyes,
And where lie the righteous, the noble, and brave,
　Till called from above to arise.

XXXII.

THE CAPTIVE.

By the wayside lay a poor bleeding stranger,
    Lone and forsaken, in anguish and pain,
Sore and oppressed—in imminent danger—
    Begging for mercy, but begging in vain.

Many pass'd by him who saw his dejection,
    Yet none in their kindness his deep wants relieved:
Both "Priest and Levite" passed by in succession,
    With cold-like indifference to the bereav'd.

Some thought him so poor, so hopelessly mangled,
    That to assist him would do him no good;
And each with the other alternately wrangled,
    What was best for him—removal or food.

Churchmen, and lawyers, and keen politicians,—
 The rich in chariots, rode by in haste;
None seemed dispos'd to shew e'en compassion
 To one, in their view, so mean and debased.

At length, one proposed for him colonization,
 Who said, "He ne'er can get well while he's
  here;
Besides, I detest an amalgamation,
 Which will be the case, as seems to appear."

While this debate was in rapid progression,
 Preacher and man-thief were found to agree:
A "fanatic" cried out, "This is oppression,—
 Heal the poor captive, and then set him free."

XXXIII.

LINES

On hearing of the Burning of the Steamer
"Lexington."

See! the boat is dashing onward,
　Through the trackless ocean, bold,
While the merry chit-chat gaily
　Echoes through her splendid hold.

But, amidst the busy concourse,
　Hark! there is a sudden cry,—
"Fire! fire! fire!—the boat's on fire!
　Oh, have mercy! must we die?"

"Where's my treasure? must I lose it?
　Where's my husband, brother, friend?
Some are burning! some are drowning!
　Ah! woe's me, is this their end?"

108   LIFE'S STRUGGLE.

 Some on bales of cotton venture—
  Others, desperate, try to leap;
 Some attempt the boats to enter,
  But are plunged into the deep.

 Still the boat is fiercely burning,
  Hopes of life for ever fled!
 One last look, and then, for ever,
  All are numbered with the dead!

XXXIV.

LIFE'S STRUGGLE.

 Life is a splendid vision,
  Short and bright;
 Then should we make provision
  To do what's right.

LIFE'S STRUGGLE.

Press onward—struggle ever,
    Work with zeal!
Time waits on mortals never—
    Life—life is real!

If we should find a creature
    Who's unbless'd,
Care-worn in every feature,
    And sore distress'd;—

Stretch forth the hand of kindness,
    And sustain,
One, who through mental blindness,
    May have been slain.

If you should find another,
    Who has need,
Ask not, "Is this my brother?"
    But help with speed.

If you can soothe his sorrow,
    Don't delay;
Stay not "until to-morrow!"—
    Haste—haste away!

Old Time is onward urging
    Every soul;
And all are swiftly verging
    On to the goal.

Therefore, be ever ready
    Thus to declare
Truth to the poor and needy,
    Everywhere.

Thought—that seems a trifle
    In its birth,
Although we partly stifle,
    May shake the earth.

LIFE'S STRUGGLE.

Then, if some thought or other
  Should leak out,
It may assist a brother,
  And ease a doubt.

One word, one pleasant feature,
  Has reliev'd
A needy fellow-creature,
  When aggriev'd!

Nature around is busy—
  Why should we
Remain contented, easy,
  Continually?

Though life is but a bubble
  Here below,
And a continual trouble
  Where'er we go,—

Yet, it hath many lessons
    To impart,
And brings a thousand blessings
    Around the heart.

Who would not do a favour,
    If he could;
And thereby help a neighbour,
    Just as he should?

Work, then, while you have power,—
    Work and wait;
Lest there should come an hour
    When it is too late.

Work for God and one another,—
    Work with zeal!
Be candid with your brother;—
    Life—life is *real!*

XXXV.

THE TREE.

This tree, this fine old tree!
    Must needs be trimm'd this year,
Its fruits, deliciously,
    Will then again appear,
And well repay the labour lent—
Besides the time we've on it spent.

This is the talk of some
    About a certain tree,
Whose very fruit alone
    Brings death and misery;
And yet they say it's fit for food,
And trim it for the nation's good.

Thus have we, many years,
    This tree of slav'ry fed,
Until its root appears
    Quite far from dead;
But rather grown so tall and great
As to have seal'd the nation's fate.

XXXVI.

ON DEATH.

O Death! thou scourge most mighty, thou!
Must all to thy dread summons bow?
Oh, stay thy coming, shield thy dart!
In thee are all to share a part?

Wilt thou respect no dignity?
Must nobles and the peasantry
Be subject to thy great command?
Insatiate, cease to scourge the land!

ON DEATH.

Thou great destroyer of our life,
Hast thou no pity for the wife,
Or husband, brother, orphan, say?
Prolong for them another day.

Consumption, palsy, plague, and pain,
Are due attendants on thy train,
Before thee go—invite thee on,
To finish what they have begun.

O Death! when shall our labour cease,
And we from terror find release?
When shall we from thy pangs be free,
And death be lost in victory?

XXXVII.

THE SLAVE'S LAMENT.

Can it be so? Has God intended
   Me to be another's slave?
To toil in anguish, undefended,
   From the cradle to the grave;
Yes, and bow my head in sorrow,
Lest I live to see the morrow?

If so, why am I not contented
   To endure this hateful chain?
Why have I constantly invented
   Schemes my liberty to gain;
And with firm, heroic brav'ry,
Ventur'd my life to flee from slav'ry?

No! God, in truth, condemns a system
    That is wretched, vile, and base;
And e'en all nature bids the victim
    Of it "fly from its embrace!"
Now, I bid adieu to slav'ry—
Its woes, its wrongs, its cunning knav'ry.

XXXVIII.

ACROSTIC.

M eekly, at an important post
O bey thy Maker—Lord!
R egardless of a scornful host,
D eclare His truth abroad.
E ndeavor to sustain the right,—
C onstant, true, and clear;
A sk Him to aid you by His might,
I n goodness persevere!

ACROSTIC.

M ake it a point to help the poor,
A nd succour the oppress'd;
N ever consent to bar their door,
N or give their tyrants rest.
A lone! you cannot be alone!
S ince truth is always nigh,
S o persevere! assur'd that One
A bove, still reigns on high!

C all'd to defend a brother's cause,
L et heart, and tongue, and pen,
A nd conscience, plead that righteous laws
R emain to govern, then
K eep thou in view the right.—Amen!

XXXIX.

HYMN,

On the Celebration of the Freedom of the West Indies.

Let's celebrate this day,
   With holy, mirthful glee,
And to the God of ages pray,
   Who set the captives free.

This day we sing Thy praise,
   And dedicate to Thee,
Because eight hundred thousand slaves
   Received their liberty!

'Twas Thy great power that wrought
   This bloodless victory;
That brought th' enslaver's pow'r to naught,
   And made Thy people free!

Their birthright now they claim,
    Free from the master's rod;
And now—in Freedom's sacred name—
    They worship only God.

Free! by Thy power divine!
    Free to enjoy Thy rest!
Free! may their hearts to Thee incline,
    And be for ever blest!

XL.

AUTUMN.

Autumn! I love thy tinted looks,
Thy fading leaves, and rippling brooks,
    And variegated flowers;
Thy cooling winds and wither'd grass,
Precursor of the stormy blast,
    And fluctuating showers.

AUTUMN.

Thy cloudy days and sultry nights,
And ripen'd fruits and pleasant sights,
    Tell, in language plain,
That thou, whose frigid looks are seen
In blighted trees, with yellow, green,
    Hath call'd on us again.

Thy varied hills and vernal plains,
Wide fields, are stock'd with ripened grains,
    And Indian summer's sun;
The crimson shadows of the sky,
And transient clouds rush swiftly by,
    And tell us, Summer's done.

The cat-bird's pensive notes, unheard,
The keen winds blow, and ev'ry bird
    Is silent through the land;
The varied foliage is seen,
Autumnal glory reigns supreme,
    Spread by Almighty hand.

AUTUMN.

Autumn! I love thy cloudy sky,
Thy many storms that pass us by,
    Thy not infrequent rain;
As ancient time still steals away
"Our years, and makes our whiskers gray,"
    Permits us to remain.

Thy annual visit and decay
Teach us a lesson, that we may
    By learning well, prepare
To live consistently below,
And be prepared, when call'd to go,
    The common fate to share.

XLI.

ODE TO DEITY.

Not unto us, but unto Thee,
  Be endless praises given,
In time and in eternity,
  On earth, and then in heaven!

For Thou art worthy to be praised
  By all that dwell above;
And saints on earth their songs have raised
  For Thy redeeming love.

Creative goodness speaks Thy power,
  While nature shows Thy skill;
And ev'ry moment—ev'ry hour—
  Proclaim Thy favour still.

If angels worship God, their King,
    And pay Him honours due,
Why should not Christians gladly sing
    To their Creator too?

Dear Lord! inspire our hearts anew,
    To run the heavenly race—
With hope and happiness in view—
    Until we see Thy face!

XLII.

GOD SPEED.

God speed the temperance cause
    Throughout this favour'd land!
May nations make their laws
    Bow to its mild command!
    Until intemperance
        No more pollutes the soil,
    But peace and competence
        Reward our toil!

Intemperance has spread—
　Its poisoned stream has run
O'er young and hoary head—
　O'er father and o'er son!
　　But since a light, not small,
　　　Has shone along our way,
　　We hope King Alcohol
　　　Has had his day!

Then let united aim,
　To save our fellow-men
From drunkenness and pain
　And degradation,—then
　　Shall men no longer be
　　　Enslaved by drinking rum,
　　But from its wiles be free
　　　All time to come!

XLIII.

ODE.

In bonds of friendship sweet,
   To soothe each other's woe,
Samaria's sons and daughters meet
   In lodges here below.

While selfishness and sin
   Cause thousands to lament,
These consecrated walls within,
   We here behold content.

By obligations bound
   Intemperance to shun,
Oh, may we constantly be found
   The enemies of rum;

And vice, and crime, and sin,
   And enmity, and pain,
Be never suffered to come in
   To mar our peace again—

Until we're called away
   To the Grand Lodge above,
And praise and adoration pay
   To purity and love.

XLIV.

THE REAPER.

There's a reaper who's been reaping
   Ever since "Old Time" began,
And he claims for his theatre,
   Earth,—and for his harvest, man!

On the battle-field he reapeth,
　By the way-side, on the sea,
Everywhere this mighty reaper
　Reapeth frail mortality.

Unlike 'most all other reapers,
　Who ne'er let their crops decay,
He reaps on, the rapid reaper
　Reaps—but lets the harvest lay.

Since this reaper began reaping,
　Millions have by him been hurl'd,
And have, from life's busy scenes, been
　Gathered—to the "spirit-world."

Though he has been constant reaping,
　Still the harvest is not done;
Whilst he passes by, he tells us
　That our reaping-time will come.

THE REAPER.

Stern and bold this reaper's reaping,
    And his locks are thin and white,
Yet he bravely wields the sickle,
    And is reaping day and night.

No distinction does this reaper
    Make—but reaps without delay;
Some of ev'ry tongue and nation
    Have by him been swept away.

If we're ready for this reaper,
    In the final deadly strife,
When the conflict's fairly over
    We shall enter into life.

XLV.

ODE.

Behold! a noble band,
United heart and hand,
    To keep from rum!
Who now stand pledg'd to save,
All men and women brave,
From the poor drunkard's grave,
    All time to come.

We raise our banners high,—
Old Alcohol defy—
    We scorn his power!
Samaria's daughters, we,
And sons, are pledged to be,
In bonds of unity,
    This sacred hour.

And in the hour of prayer
We feel each other's care
    In friendship bind.
And now and ever more
The wounded we'll restore,
And feed and clothe the poor
    Of all mankind.

In this, our humble sphere,
While thus we journey here,
    We'll raise our voice,
And with a noble shout,
We'll find the drunkard out,
And turn him right about,
    And then rejoice!

Our "Grand Master" on high,
Who reigns triumphantly,
    And dwells above,

Bids us go on, and bind
The worst of human kind—
The poor, the halt, the blind—
    With cords of love.

Then, when our work is done,
When the last sand is run,
    When we're no more;
Then may our sentence be—
"Thou hast done faithfully,
Enter eternity,
    Thy God adore!"

XLVI.

FORGET THEE.

Forget thee! no, not I indeed—
    The time appears as yesterday,
And thoughts bring back again with speed
    The simple words we used to say.

FORGET THEE.

Forget thee! no, I cannot while
    I think, and reason doth its part,
Thy features—form—thy very smile,
    Have made an impress on my heart.

Forget thee! yes, indeed I may,
    When nature withers through neglect,
And sun grows dim, and stars decay;
    Not until then can I forget.

Forget thee! can I? surely not;
    Until all things shall cease to be;
Till earth itself shall be forgot,
    And time breaks in eternity.

XLVII.

TO WRITE.

Upon being asked to write in an Album by Miss A. C. C.

To write in your "Album" I am not inclined,
   Although I no reason can give,
Unless I should tell you I scarce have a mind
   To utter a thought that should live.

But since you insist, I suppose I must try—
   So here goes to do what I can,
Why, bless me! my thoughts have this moment gone by—
   The truants, how swiftly they ran!

TO WRITE. 135

To write right, the right way would be to
   write well,
  Yet who can write well without thought?
And if the right thoughts will for ever rebel,
  How can I write right as I ought?

Then how can I write in your "Album," dear
   Miss,
  If fugitive thoughts will not stay?
I hope you'll excuse an occasion like this—
  So, therefore, I bid you good-day.

But stay,—I should wonder, can thoughts run
   away
  From one who never had any?
This problem I leave you to solve as you may,
  Your "Album" will solve it to many.

XLVIII.

LINES

On the Death of a Child, J. W., aged 11 years.

Like a transient shining light,
    From beneath a cloudless sky,
Like a swift-wing'd seraph bright,
    Thou hast gone to realms on high.

Though so few thy days on earth,
    And affliction held thee fast,
Yet thou knew'st the second birth
    Ere eleven years had past.

Testimony thou didst leave,
    Seldom heard from infant's tongue;
Father, mother, do not grieve
    For my loss, although so young.

Mother, do not angels sing?
   Oh! I long with them to be,
Praising God, my Saviour King;
   Mother, will not you meet me,—

Meet me where the weary rest,
   Where affliction is unknown,
Where the saints of God are bless'd:
   Meet me round my Father's throne?

XLIX.

WHO HATH COURAGE?

Who hath courage? Not the hero
   Leading in the strife,
To receive a nation's plaudits,
   For his waste of life.

Who, then, is it that hath courage?
    He alone who dares
Act up to his own convictions,
    And the right declares.

Who hath courage? Not the tyrant
    Boasting of his skill,
To enslave and bind his fellow
    At his simple will.

Who, then, is it that hath courage?
    He that doth proclaim,
Unto all their right to freedom,
    Every man the same.

Who hath courage? Not the sober,
    Or untempted one,
Who hath never had his stomach
    Eaten out by rum.

Who, then, is it that hath courage?
    He who though he may
Have been using poison freely,
    Throws the cup away.

Who hath courage? Not the daring,
    Reckless pugilist,
Who for wager smites a brother,
    With uplifted fist.

Who, then, is it that hath courage?
    He that won t resent
Every little insult given
    With a base intent.

L.

YEARS.

AFTER a few short years
  Our race will have been run;
This short probation given us
  Will end beneath the sun.

LI.

CHEER UP.

CHEER up, brother; why dejected?
  Pain will cease and sorrows end.
Why discourag'd if neglected?
  Just look upwards, there's a friend.

Cheer up, brother; there's a power
  That upholds when none is near;
And through all life's darkest hour
  Whispers sweetly—do not fear.

CHEER UP.

Cheer up, brother; though the mountain
    May be rugged, rough, and high,
From its apex flows a fountain;
    Slake your thirst whenever dry.

Cheer up, brother; though oppression
    Stalketh boldly hand in hand,
Girt with truth—keep self-possession,
    Thou shalt reach a better land.

Cheer up, brother; in the distance
    May be seen a single star,
All throughout life's poor existence,
    See it, brightly beaming there.

Cheer up, brother; angels hover
    All around you in the strife,
With their golden pinions cover
    O'er the path to endless life.

Cheer up, brother; don't be fearful
   Though the raging billows roar,
Full of hope and faith, be cheerful,
   There are millions on before.

Cheer up, brother; why thus slumber?
   Battle manfully and brave;
There is yet an untold number
   That in mercy Christ will save.

LII.

THE PAUPER'S GRAVE.

No friend to wipe the sweat of death
      From off his face,
Or kindred, when he drew his breath
      In this deserted place.

THE PAUPER'S GRAVE.

So, here he lies beneath the soil,
>> Where wild weeds grow,
The poor, the pauper, freed from toil,
>> In rough-hewn boxes low.

No marble monument to tell,
>> In doubtful truth,
That he had acted ill or well
>> In hoary age or youth.

A simple board is all that's seen,
>> Or points to where
In silence sleeps the poor plebeian,
>> Releas'd from earthly care.

LIII.

THE CRISIS.

When a crisis heaves in view,
    Manfully meet it;
Do not shrink or be dismay'd,
    Cheerfully greet it.

All dangers mostly end by
    Strong opposition;
Then take a noble stand, and
    A firm position.

Like trees whose roots are deep, and
    Whose branches flowing,
Firmly resist the shock, while
    The storm is blowing.

THE CRISIS.

Then be not recreant, and
    Do not disemble,
And when the crisis comes, like
    A coward tremble.

Clouds that are threatening, and
    Fill us with sorrow,
Oft bring a blessing on with
    The early morrow.

Then manfully resist, with
    A firm reliance;
Trusting to Providence, meet
    It with defiance.

LIV.

AN ACROSTIC.

W e have seen thee, years ago,
I n our early manhood days,
L ighting up a world below,
L ike a comet in full blaze.
I nto Slav'ry's dark abode
A ll the fire of truth was sent;
M any trembl'd at the word,

L ike an aspen tree when bent.
O nward—is thy motto still,
Y oung and old have follow'd thee,
E v'n almost against their will,
D riv'n to plead for liberty.

G o on pleading for the dumb,
A lthough held forth as a knave;
R eckless thou art call'd by some,
R ob'd in truth, be valiant—brave.
I f thou can'st not live to see
S lav'ry from this nation driv'n,
O h! may'st thou rewarded be,
N ot on earth, but high in heav'n.

LV.

REQUIESCAT IN PACE.

On the Death of Caroline Millen Clark, who
Died 1st December, 1857.

Just like a rose in early spring,
    That blooms and withers in a day;
So thou, poor fragile sickly thing,
        Was early call'd away.

REQUIESCAT IN PACE.

'Tis hard indeed to bid farewell
  To one belov'd, so young and mild;
None but a parent's heart can tell
    The love he bears his child.

We stood around thy dying bed,
  We heard thee offer up a prayer
Unto thy Father God; who said,—
    Come, and my kingdom share.

We know that thou art call'd away,
  But, ah! 'tis hard with thee to part;
It breaks the tender ties that lay
    Entwined around the heart.

'Twas in the budding time of life,
  Ere crime had made its deadly stain,
Thou left a world of sin and strife,
    In heaven above to reign.

A little while, then, Caroline,
   In that bright world we'll meet again,
Where, like the sun, thou shalt outshine,
     Among the holy train.

LVI.

PILGRIM.

Pilgrim on the toilsome way,
   Through this vale of sorrow,
There will be a better day,
   Wrestle till the morrow.

Say not that your trouble's great,
   Or your conflicts many;
On your Heavenly Father wait,
   He doth succour any.

All the holy righteous dead,
    All the martyrs bleeding,
Are but just gone on a-head,
    Press on—never heeding.

They through blood have struggled on,
    Through the flames and fire;
But they now can look upon
    Jesus, and admire.

Are you tempted to look back,
    Give the struggle over?
Think of those who, on the rack,
    Prais'd the great Jehovah.

Pilgrim on the toilsome way,
    Through this vale of sorrow,
Surely there's a better day,
    There's a brighter morrow.

LVII.

NO ENERGY.

In all my life I never knew
   A creature to do well without it.
What! have no energy to do,
   And yet succeed?—I really doubt it.

Then why sit down at ease and say—
   "This can't be done, that, or the other:"
In such a man I have no faith,
   No matter who may be his mother.

What think ye of the farmer who
   Neglects to sow his grain in season,
And yet expects to reap the fruit
   In time;—think ye he acts with reason?

NO ENERGY.

The man of energy will dare
    To do what suits his will or pleasure;
Though thousands all around him fail,
    Yet he secures the honoured treasure.

'Tis energy that guides the plough,
    And makes the steamer roar and rattle,
Directs the ship in every port,
    And makes the hero dare in battle.

In all my life I never knew
    The energetic man to stumble,
Or, if he fails in one attempt,
    To sit down and begin to grumble.

"What man has done may yet," he cries,
    "Be done by man in any station;
So I will try, and try again,
    And bid defiance to the nation."

LVIII.

ACROSTIC, A. C. C.

A lthough possess'd of youth and health,
L et not vain thoughts abound,
M idst every flower, as by stealth,
I nsects will oft be found.
R emember then—remember when
A ll things in time will fail,

C oolly survey the future, then
R egard this earth as frail.
A ges have proved this saying true,
N or can it be denied,
D espite of all that men can do,
E vil will flow from pride;
L et meekness guide your course through life,
Love, virtue, truth, and grace.

C almly avoid all needless strife,
L eading you to disgrace,
A lmira—this I bid you do,
R espect yourself, the right pursue;
K eep this advice always in view.

LIX.

AN EPITAPH

ON MY DOG TURK.

The last remains of "Turk" lie here,
Who ne'er was known to shrink, or fear
      The face of interloper;
Poor "Turk" was ever, soon or late,
From puppy up to dog's estate,
      A foe to thief or loafer.

So thus upon a certain day,
As "Turk" stole out, some thought to play,
      Or to hide from his master,

Oh, cruel fate! he was shot dead;
The ball pass'd through the poor dog's head—
      Such was his sad disaster.

Now, all the canine race may take
Warning by "Turk's" unhappy fate,
      And learn to stay at home;
Nor bark or bite, and snarl and scout,
Or break their chains and run about,
      When call'd, refuse to come.

LX.

DO THEY MISS ME?

A PARODY.

"Do they miss me at home—do they miss me?"
  'Twould be an assurance to me,
To know that I'm really forgotten,
  My face they could never more see.

"Do they miss me at home—do they miss me?"
  By light, as the horn echoes loud,
And the slaves are marched off to the corn-field,
  I 'm miss'd from that half-naked crowd.

"Do they miss me at home—do they miss me?"
  The hut, with its bare floor of dirt,
Where the ash-cake is waiting to greet me,
  When done with my thankless day's work.

"Do they miss me at home—do they miss me?"
  The driver his lash used to ply,
As the blood trickl'd down from my shoulders
  The flesh from my body would fly.

"Do they miss me at home—do they miss me?"
  The blood-hounds are scenting my track,
And for long weary days they have hunted,
  In order to hurry me back.

"Do they miss me at home—do they miss me?"
  The pockets are empty of cash,
While the auction-block's waiting to meet me
  The trader stands by with his lash.

"Do they miss me at home—do they miss me?"
  In the fields of rice, sugar, and grain;
If they do, I am glad, I assure you,
  They never shall see me again.

LXI.

GOSSIP!

Oh! Mrs. A——, have you not heard
  The news around the town?
'Tis said that Mr. B—— was seen
  To look at Mrs. Brown!

Then Mr. C——, I really heard,—
  Don't tell it for your life,—
Has just determin'd, only think,
  To make Miss D—— his wife!

And Mr. E—— is going to—
  I promis'd not to tell—
Be married to Miss F——, down street;
  'Tis thought that she'll do well.

The news is now, that young Miss G——
  Is dead in love with H——;
But now, they say, he does not care,
  He's courting Sally Baich.

I—— call'd on me the other day,
  And ask'd me if I could
Speak a good word for him to J——;
  But do you think I would?

Why, there is K——, that prims so much,
  And dresses very gay;
They tell me she's engag'd to L——,
  But I doubt all they say!

What do you think of M——'s new coat?
   N—— says it don't look well.
Dear me! what makes O—— flirt so much?
   That P——'s a perfect swell!

Q—— call'd on me the other day,
   And ask'd me what I thought
Of the new dress that R—— had on,
   The other day she bought.

The bonnet that Miss S—— had on,
   They said, came o'er the sea;
But young Miss T—— said U—— told her,
   'Twas bought up town of V——.

W—— thinks so much of X——,
   Y—— says Z——'s lips are down!
And now I've told you all the news
   There is around the town.

LXII.

LOVE.

Oh! gentle sir, calm and secure,
    Lone on your pillow wake,
A lady, knocking at your door,
    Has brought her heart to break.

That heart is offer'd to you now;
    Will you accept the prize,
Or disregard love's open vow,
    And hide it from your eyes?

Ah, gentle sir! love's not a dream
    Of fancied vision bright;
But rather like a limpid stream
    That's running day and night.

'Tis like a precious gem that lay
    Within the earth conceal'd,
Until the mighty orb of day
    Its beauties hath reveal'd.

LXIII.

ON THE TIMES.

See the prancing steed is foaming,
    Eager to enjoy the strife;
As it is in exact keeping
    With the habits of his life.

With the blood up to the bridle,
    He is coursing o'er the plain;
And the fields are thickly lying
    With the bodies of the slain.

Men engaged in deadly conflict,
    Who did heretofore agree,
Brother against brother striving,
    Desperate, yet ignobly.

Why are men thus in confusion,
    Scarcely dreaming what they do,
Arming to engage a foeman,
    Yet not really knowing who?

Are they making preparation
    For a future deadly blow—
The great work of "Armageddon"
    To be fought on earth below?

Where the birds shall all be gather'd,
    To enjoy a feast of God;
And the nations will be smitten
    By His dire avenging rod.

These are surely times of trouble;
    Men are fill'd with dread dismay,
Looking for what shall transpire,
    At some future coming day,

When this planet shall be purged
    Of its dross, its sin, and shame,
And the "King" possess the kingdom,
    And "a thousand years shall reign."

LXIV.

MEET IN HEAVEN.

Ah! shall we meet at last in heav'n,
　　As here on earth we meet;
And there, redeem'd, with sins forgiv'n,
　　Each other kindly greet?

What! meet in heav'n, where Jesus reigns,
　　In that resplendent sphere?
It will repay for all the pains
　　And cares we suffer'd here.

We'll meet in heav'n if faithful, when
　　These troublous times are o'er;
Oh! yes, we'll meet in heav'n again,
　　As we've met heretofore.

It stands engrav'd in solid brass,
   And to His people giv'n,
A promise, that if true at last
   They all shall meet in heav'n.

"Unto the swift is not the race,"
   Nor battle to the strong;
But he who treads the path of grace,
   The journey all along.

To him the prize is freely giv'n,
   Who struggles to the end;
He shall enjoy a rest in heav'n,
   A rest with Christ his friend.

LXV.

BE JOYFUL!

Dedicated to the First Colored Regiment
of Michigan.

Two years gone by, then we were told,
    We do not want your aid;
Our fighting—all we mean to do,
    And dying, too, 'twas said.
Now truth maintains her ancient strife
    With slavery, loud and long;
In deadly grasp they struggle on,
    Till right shall conquer wrong.

Chorus—

Oh! it will be joyful, joyful, joyful;
Oh! it will he joyful, when slavery is no more,
When slavery is no more, when slavery is no more;
Then we'll sing, and offering bring, when slavery is no more.

The wolverenes of Michigan,
  The coloured first—though new,
Will boldly to the contest march,
  And strike for freedom too.
With Millican, Port Hudson, and
  Fort Waggoner in view,
We'll bleed and die for liberty,
  As freemen only do.
    Chorus—Oh! that will be joyful, &c.

To make our country what it should,
  Has always been of right;
A land of just and equal laws,
  And not of force and might:
A place where not a fetter'd slave
  Shall ever clank his chain;
But where, without regard to caste,
  Freedom and truth shall reign.
    Chorus—Oh! it will be joyful, &c.

BE JOYFUL. 167

What then shall our status be,
    And victory shall be won,   [flag,
When marked, and scarred, with tattered
    We from the battle come?
We care not what we then shall be,
    For if we 're true and brave,
Be what we will, with arms in hand,
    We won't be made a slave.
        Chorus—Oh! it will be joyful, &c.

We fight for God and liberty,
    For justice, truth, and right,
The freedom of the helpless slave
    Against the tyrant's might.
We do not doubt which will succeed
    In such a cause as this;
The bullets of a freeman's arm
    Were never known to miss.
        Chorus—Oh! it will be joyful, &c.

We've heard from Louisiana,
　　The Bay State, and from Penn,
And last—not least—here come the sons
　　Of good old Michigan.
And now three cheers for ————,
　　Who has the soldiers made,
And three loud groans for copperheads
　　Who will not lend their aid.
　　　　　Chorus—Oh! it will be joyful, &c.